SANTA'S COLORING AND ACTIVITY BOOK™

KAPPA Books

Visit us at www.kappapublishing.com/kappabooks

Copyright ©2010 by Kappa Books Publishers, LLC.
No part of this book may be reproduced or copied without written permission of the publisher.
All rights reserved. Printed in the UNITED STATES OF AMERICA.

W9-CAW-862

Connect the dots.

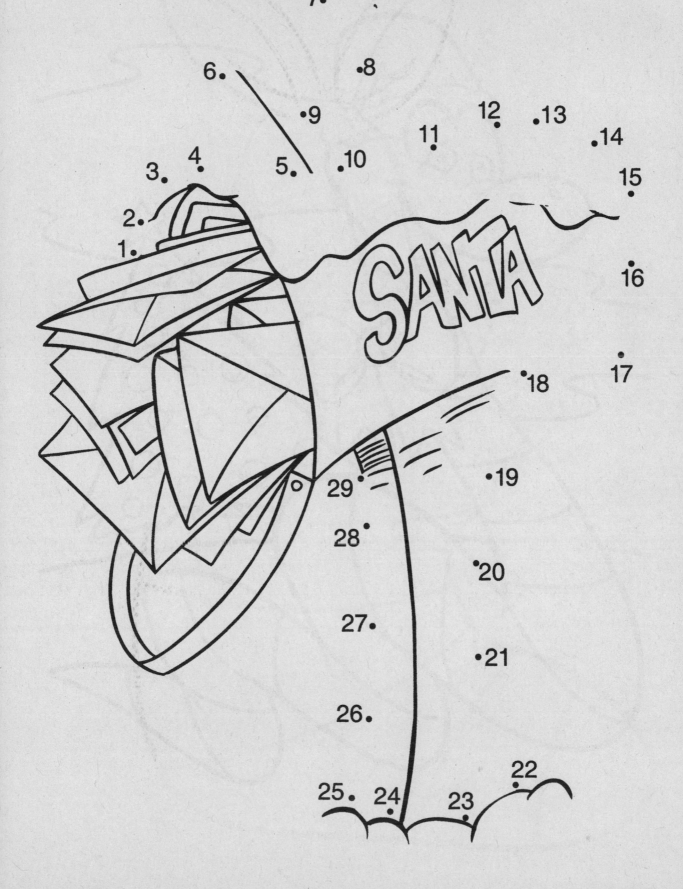

Word-Find

Find and circle the
words in the puzzle.

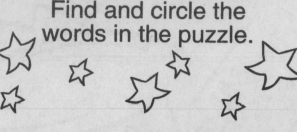

S P O C E S G Q P N B
K A R A Y U B I B C L
J D N S Z C L E F L E
S U A K D O A M S T Y
U B M E H O H Q T A S
R W E I S K L S R T L
P A N L T I C L G E E
R Y T A L E K I S R I
I P W T Q S W O U S G
S E A S T A R S R Y H
E L I F R I E N D S F

1. GIFTS	4. FRIENDS	7. STARS
2. ORNAMENT	5. COOKIES	8. SURPRISE
3. SLEIGH	6. BELLS	9. DOLLS

Finish the picture of Santa.

WHICH IS DIFFERENT?

Can you find the picture that is different?

1.

2.

3.

4.

5.

MAZE

See if you can find your way through the maze.

Start

Finish

Color By Letter

Use the color chart
below to color
the picture.

A=Green B=White C=Orange D=Pink E=Red F=Black

WHICH IS DIFFERENT?

Can you find the picture that is different?

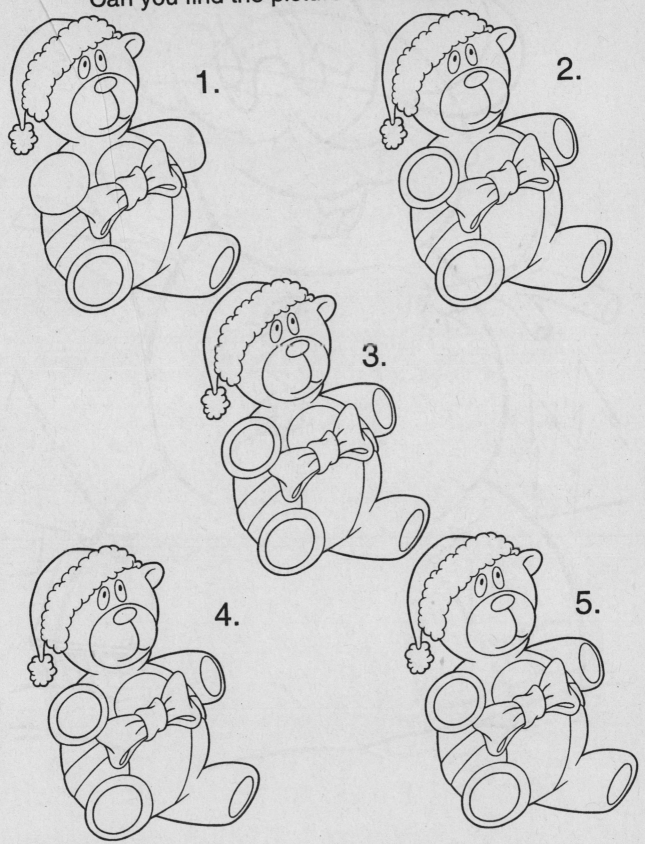

1.

2.

3.

4.

5.

How many words can you make out of
DECORATIONS?

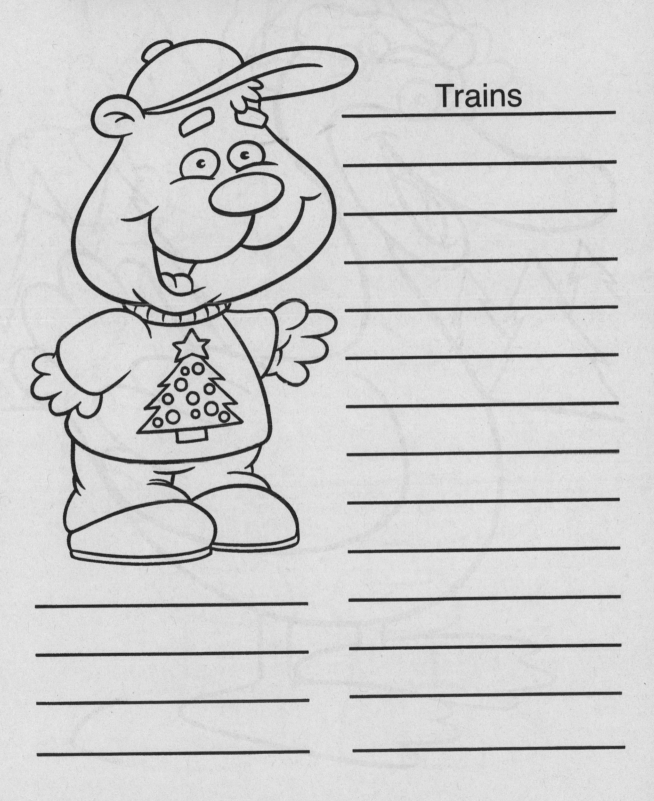

Trains

SECRET MESSAGE

Use the code at left to solve the message.

A=26
B=25
C=24
D=23
E=22
F=21
G=20
H=19
I=18
J=17
K=16
L=15
M=14
N=13
O=12
P=11
Q=10
R=9
S=8
T=7
U=6
V=5
W=4
X=3
Y=2
Z=1

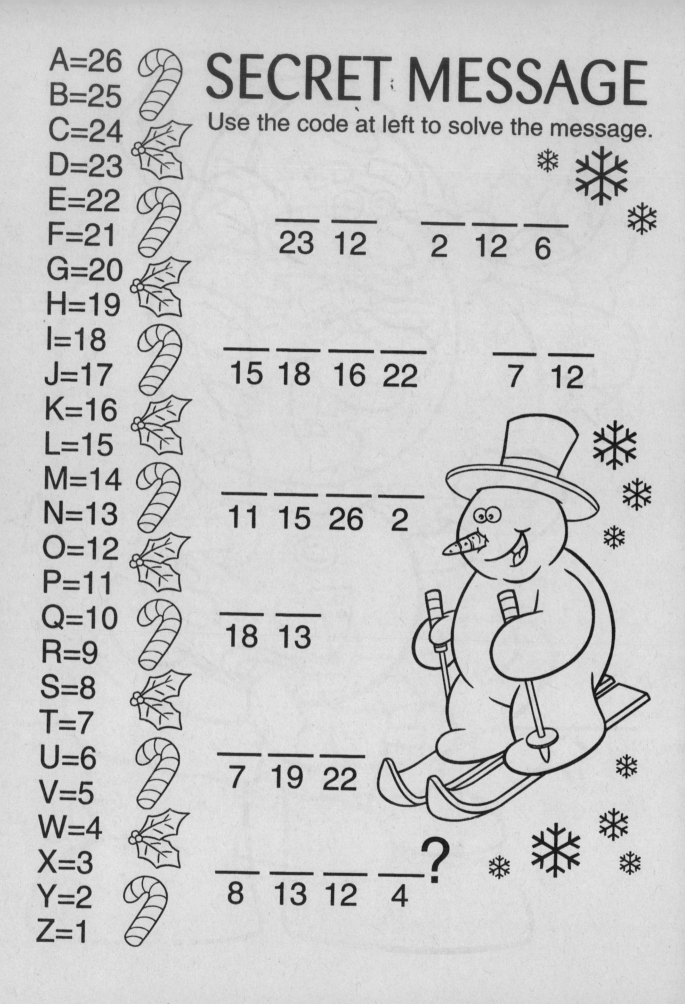

__ __ __ __ __
23 12 2 12 6

__ __ __ __   __ __
15 18 16 22   7 12

__ __ __ __
11 15 26 2

__ __
18 13

__ __ __
7 19 22

__ __ __ __?
8 13 12 4

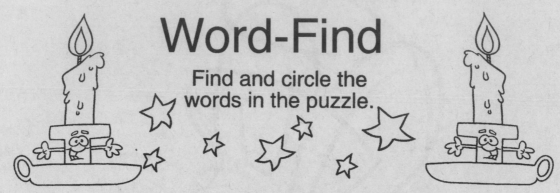

Word-Find

Find and circle the
words in the puzzle.

```
S  P  A  R  T  I  E  S  P  N  B
K  N  P  S  H  A  R  I  N  G  R
J  D  O  S  O  N  C  E  R  L  E
T  G  J  W  B  A  E  M  S  U  I
I  S  I  E  M  B  G  I  R  S  N
E  Q  L  V  F  A  G  S  I  T  D
G  E  Q  B  I  C  N  S  B  A  E
B  L  R  A  P  N  O  I  B  W  E
C  V  W  T  L  U  G  A  O  S  R
P  E  P  P  E  R  M  I  N  T  A
P  S  I  A  T  Q  D  G  D  X  F
```

1. SNOWMAN
2. EGGNOG
3. PEPPERMINT
4. GIVING
5. PARTIES
6. RIBBON
7. SHARING
8. REINDEER
9. ELVES

How many words can you make out of
CANDY CANE?

Day _____

_____

_____

_____

_____

_____

_____

_____

_____

_____   _____

_____   _____

_____   _____

_____   _____

Draw
decorations
on the
tree!

W IC IS DIFFE E T?

Can you find the picture that is different?

WHICH IS DIFFERENT?

Can you find the picture that is different?

1.

2.

3.

4.

5.

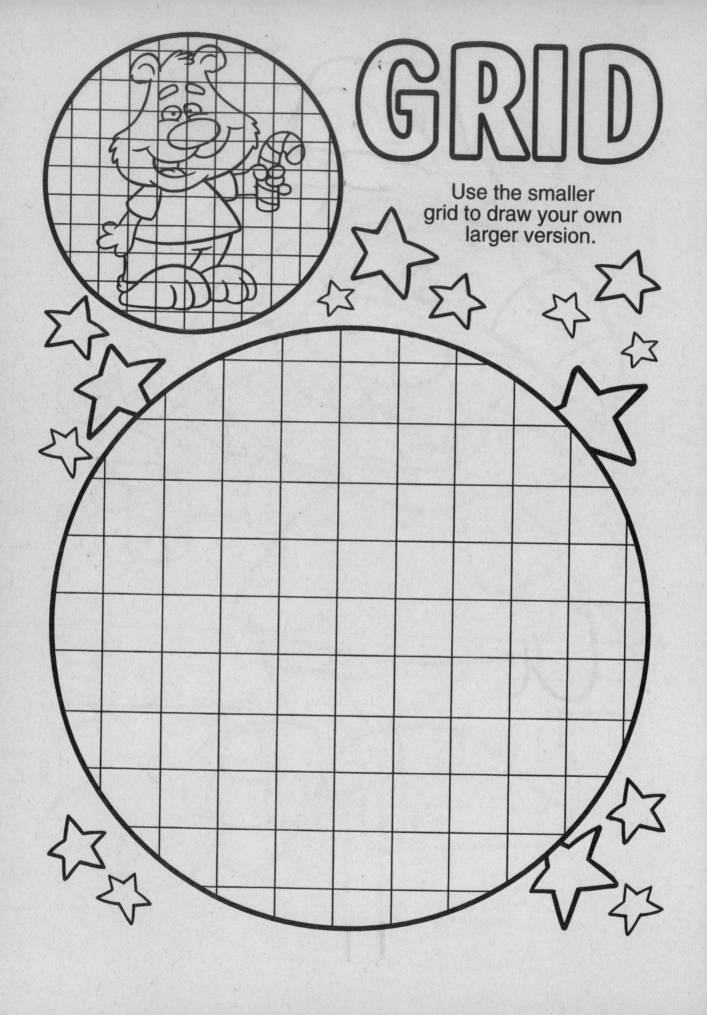

GRID

Use the smaller
grid to draw your own
larger version.

MAZE

See if you can find your
way through the maze.

Start

Finish

Write a letter to Santa.

WHICH IS DIFFERENT?

Can you find the picture that is different?

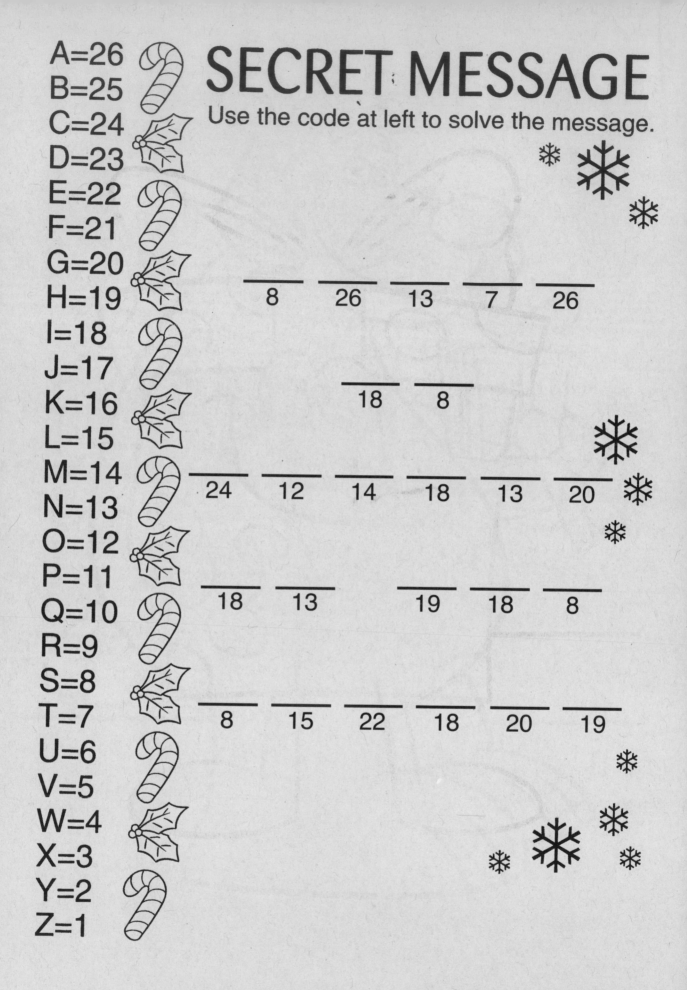

SECRET MESSAGE
Use the code at left to solve the message.

A=26
B=25
C=24
D=23
E=22
F=21
G=20
H=19
I=18
J=17
K=16
L=15
M=14
N=13
O=12
P=11
Q=10
R=9
S=8
T=7
U=6
V=5
W=4
X=3
Y=2
Z=1

8   26   13   7   26

18   8

24   12   14   18   13   20

18   13   19   18   8

8   15   22   18   20   19

Color by letter.

Use the color chart below to color the picture.

A=Flesh B=Blue C=Green D=Black E=Red F=Yellow

Color by letter.

Use the color chart below to color the picture.

A=Purple B=Pink C=Green D=White E=Red F=Yellow

WHICH IS DIFFERENT?

Can you find the picture that is different?

1.

2.

3.

4.

5.

Connect the dots.

Finish the
picture of the
snowman.

Decorate and color the cookies.

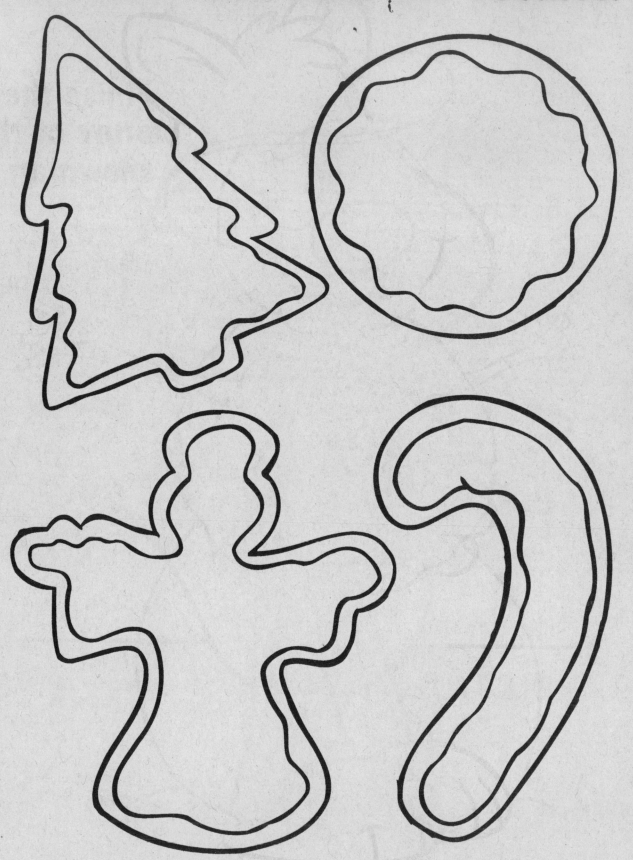

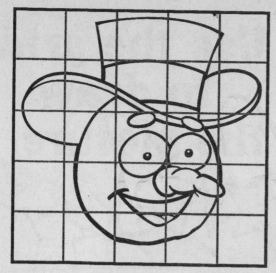

Use the grid to draw the picture.

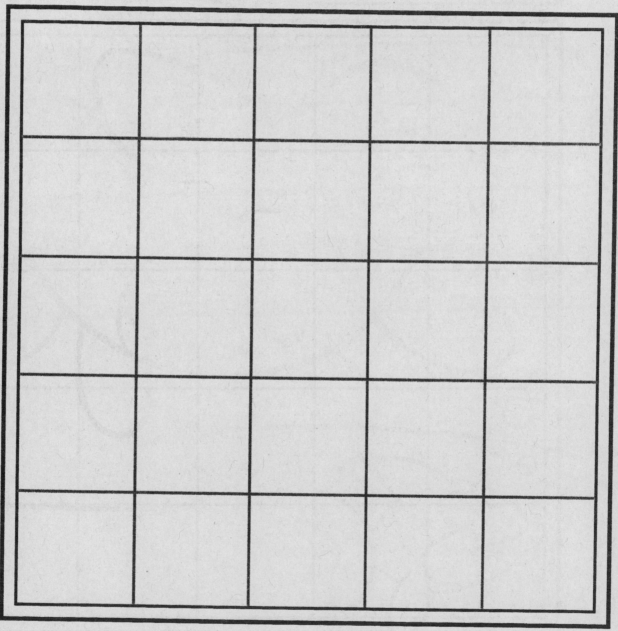

Use the grid to draw the picture.

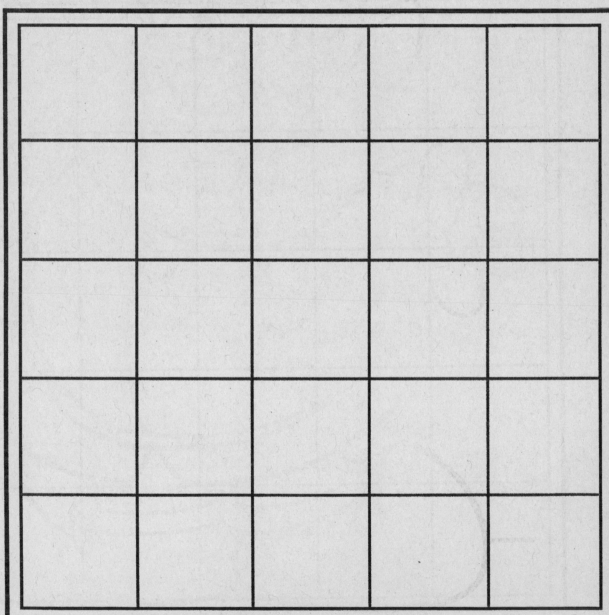

Answers

Dot-to-Dot

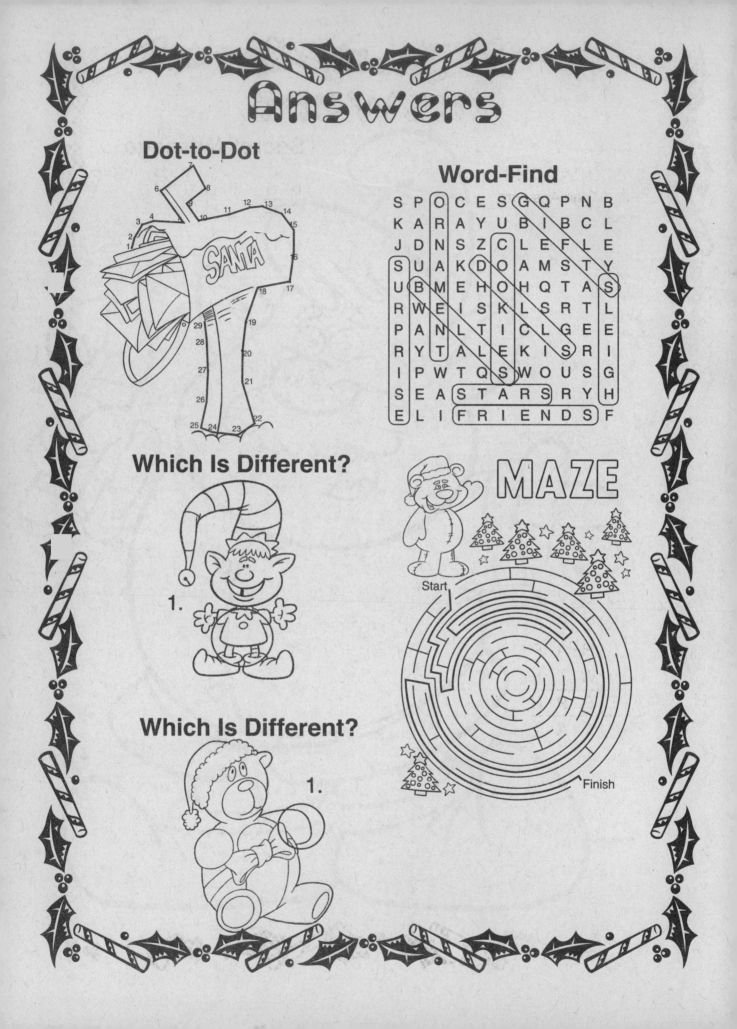

Word-Find

```
S P O C E S G Q P N B
K A R A Y U B I B C L
J D N S Z C L E F L E
S U A K D O A M S T Y
U B M E H O H Q T A S
R W E I S K L S R T L
P A N L T I C L G E E
R Y T A L E K I S R I
I P W T Q S W O U S G
S E A S T A R S R Y H
E L I F R I E N D S F
```

Which Is Different?

1.

Which Is Different?

1.

MAZE

Start

Finish

Answers

DECORATIONS

Suggested Answers:

Race
Tin
Rat
Corn
Stair
Crate
Sat
Door
Root
Ton

Secret Message

D O   Y O U ❄❄
23 12   2 12 6

L I K E   T O
15 18 16 22   7 12

P L A Y
11 15 26 2

I N
18 13

T H E
7 19 22

S N O W ?
8 13 12 4

Word-Find

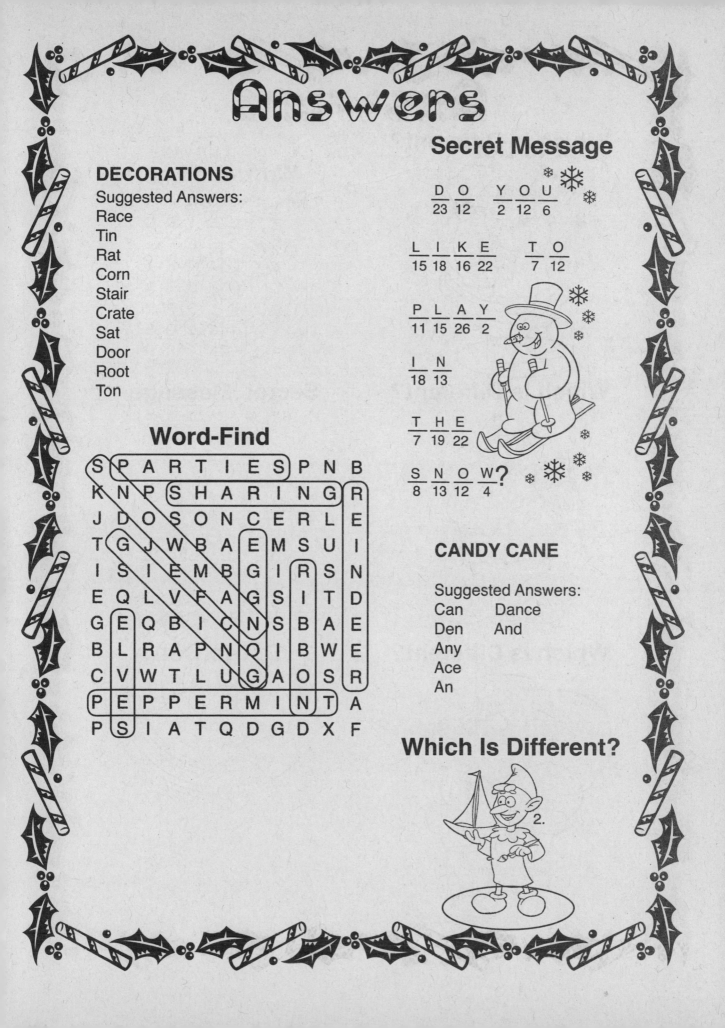

```
S P A R T I E S P N B
K N P S H A R I N G R
J D O S O N C E R L E
T G J W B A E M S U I
I S I E M B G I R S N
E Q L V F A G S I T D
G E Q B I C N S B A E
B L R A P N O I B W E
C V W T L U G A O S R
P E P P E R M I N T A
P S I A T Q D G D X F
```

CANDY CANE

Suggested Answers:

Can	Dance
Den	And
Any	
Ace	
An	

Which Is Different?

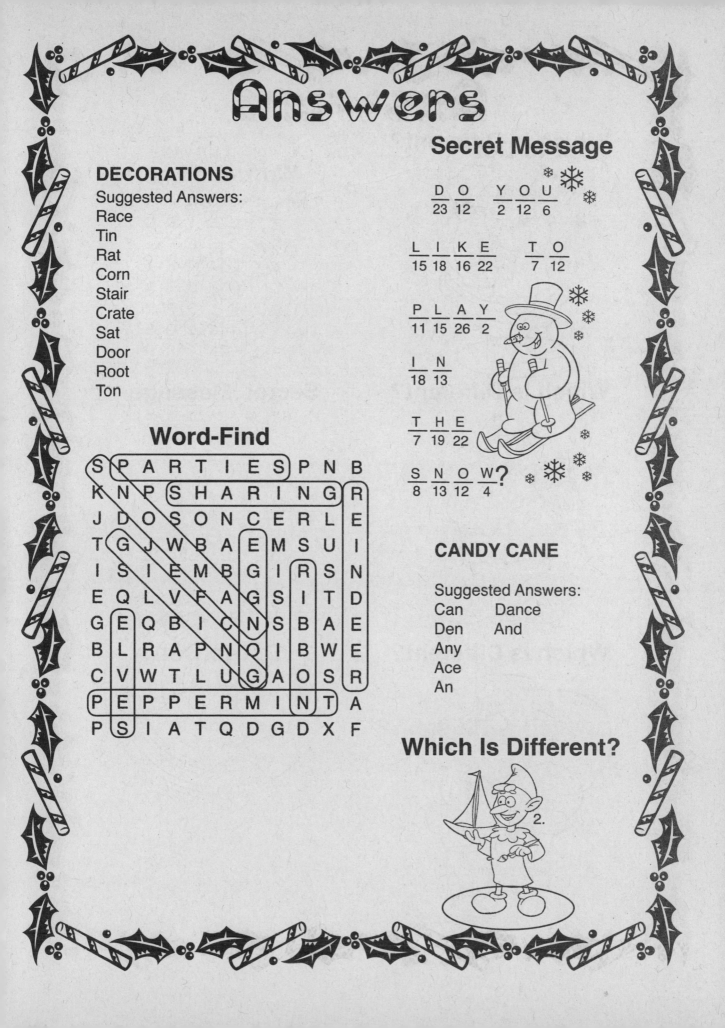

2.

Answers

Which Is Different?

3.

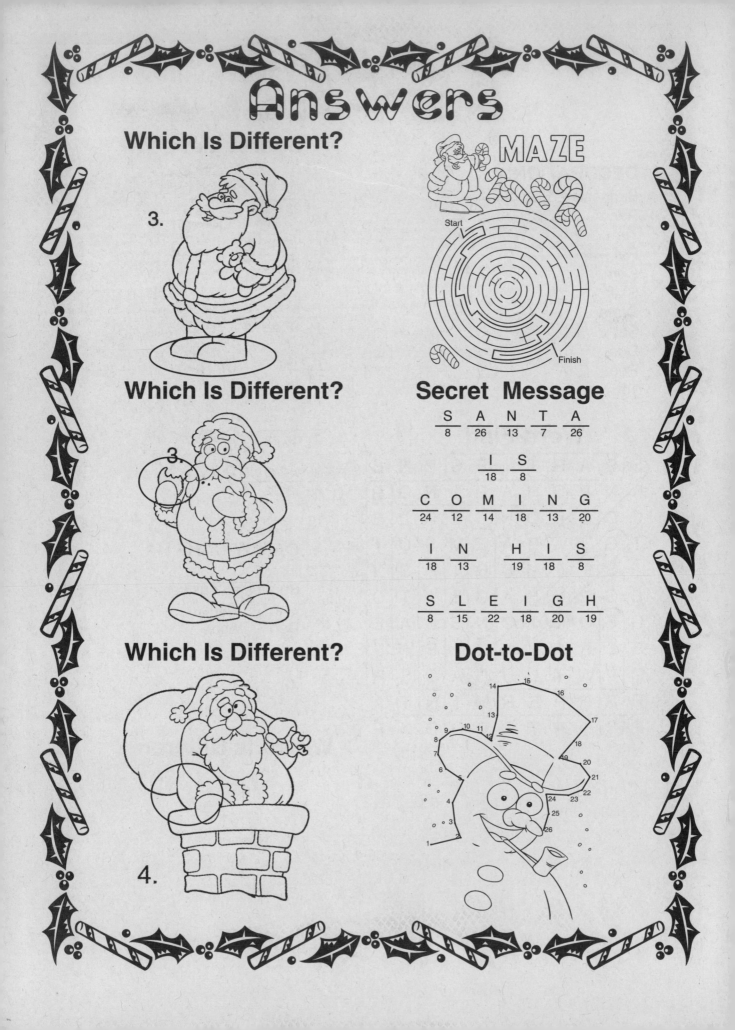

MAZE

Start

Finish

Which Is Different?

3

Secret Message

$\underset{8}{S}$ $\underset{26}{A}$ $\underset{13}{N}$ $\underset{7}{T}$ $\underset{26}{A}$

$\underset{18}{I}$ $\underset{8}{S}$

$\underset{24}{C}$ $\underset{12}{O}$ $\underset{14}{M}$ $\underset{18}{I}$ $\underset{13}{N}$ $\underset{20}{G}$

$\underset{18}{I}$ $\underset{13}{N}$ $\underset{19}{H}$ $\underset{18}{I}$ $\underset{8}{S}$

$\underset{8}{S}$ $\underset{15}{L}$ $\underset{22}{E}$ $\underset{18}{I}$ $\underset{20}{G}$ $\underset{19}{H}$

Which Is Different?

Dot-to-Dot

4.